MONEY MARKET FUNDS INVESTING 101

A Beginner's Guide to Building Financial Security

Usiere Uko

ISBN-13: 979-8-253-62982-6

SECOND EDITION

...To new frontiers, learning and growing

CONTENTS

INTRODUCTION

THE BEGINNER'S SMART INVESTORS GUIDE TO BUILDING FINANCIAL SECURITY

I f you find yourself struggling to save money and constantly dipping into your savings for expenses, you're not alone. It can be challenging to find a place to put your money where it can grow and work for you instead of being spent impulsively. That's where investing in a Money Market Fund can make a significant difference.

Welcome to this book, designed to be your comprehensive guide in exploring and benefiting from the world of money market funds. We will take you on a journey towards understanding the power of money market funds and how they can help you build a stable financial future.

In today's rapidly changing financial landscape, finding the right investment avenues can be a daunting task. As a beginner investor, you might feel overwhelmed by the myriad of options available, unsure about where to start, or concerned about the risks involved. Fear not, for you have picked up this book, and we are here to guide you every step of the way.

This book is crafted with a clear purpose: to empower you with the knowledge and confidence needed to navigate the world of money market funds with ease. Whether you're a college student looking to save for future expenses, a young professional seeking to build an emergency fund, or someone preparing for retirement, money market funds can play a crucial role in helping you achieve your financial goals.

In the following chapters, we will embark on a comprehensive journey through the fundamentals of money market funds, their mechanics, benefits, and risks. You'll learn how these funds work, their investment strategies, and how they fit into your broader financial plan.

Throughout this guide, we'll address your concerns and answer your questions. Worried about the risks? We'll delve into that and show you how to make informed decisions that align with your risk tolerance. Confused about taxes and how they impact your investments? We've got you covered with a dedicated chapter on that subject.

By the end of this book, you'll be equipped with the tools to confidently select the right money market fund for your needs, maximize returns, and manage potential risks effectively. The goal is to empower you to take control of your financial future and build lasting financial security.

Investing is not just about growing your money; it's about making smart decisions that align with your goals and values. As we explore money market funds together, we'll emphasize the importance of a well-balanced financial strategy, diversification, and prudent risk management.

So, let's embark on this enriching journey together. Whether you are a novice investor or someone looking to expand your financial knowledge, this book is tailored to meet you where you are and guide you toward greater financial prosperity.

Get ready to explore the world of money market funds and embark on a path toward financial security. Let's dive in and make your money work harder for you.

PART 1: UNDERSTANDING MONEY MARKET FUNDS

1: WHAT ARE MONEY MARKET FUNDS?

L et's start by laying the foundation for understanding money market funds, giving you a clear grasp of what they are, how they work, and the unique role they play in the world of investments. By the end of this chapter, you'll have a deep understanding of what money market funds are, how they operate, and the invaluable position they hold in the investment landscape.

DEFINITION AND OVERVIEW OF MONEY MARKET FUNDS:

Money market funds are a type of mutual fund that aims to provide investors with a safe and stable place to park their cash while earning a modest return. These funds invest in short-term, high-quality, and low-risk debt instruments, such as Treasury bills, commercial paper, certificates of deposit, and other money market instruments.

The primary objective of money market funds is capital preservation, making them an attractive option for individuals and organizations seeking safety and liquidity for their excess cash reserves. While they are not designed to generate significant returns like riskier investments, they offer a convenient and low-risk way to earn a modest yield on your cash.

HOW MONEY MARKET FUNDS DIFFER FROM OTHER TYPES OF INVESTMENTS

Money market funds stand apart from other investment options in several key ways:

Risk Profile: Money market funds are considered low-risk investments compared to stocks or long-term bonds. They are subject to fewer fluctuations in value and are less susceptible to market volatility.

Investment Horizon: Money market funds are designed for short-term investing, typically with maturities ranging from a few days to one year. This makes them ideal for investors with short-term financial goals or those looking to maintain liquidity.

Return Potential: While money market funds provide more stability, their return potential is generally lower than other riskier asset classes. The focus here is on capital preservation and liquidity rather than chasing high returns.

Liquidity: One of the significant advantages of money market funds is their high level of liquidity. Investors can typically access their funds quickly, often with no penalties, making them an excellent option for emergency funds or short-term cash needs.

THE ROLE OF MONEY MARKET FUNDS IN A BALANCED PORTFOLIO:

When building a well-diversified investment portfolio, money market funds play a crucial role in maintaining stability and liquidity (financial security portfolio). While they may not be the primary source of growth in a portfolio, they serve as a safe haven during periods of market volatility.

Money market funds offer a place to park cash temporarily while investors assess other investment opportunities or wait for more favorable market conditions. Additionally, they serve as a buffer against market downturns, providing a source of capital that can be used to take advantage of attractive investment opportunities when they arise.

By allocating a portion of your investment portfolio to money market funds, you can strike a balance between preserving capital, generating income, and participating in growth-oriented assets. This diversification can help reduce overall portfolio risk and improve the chances of achieving your long-term financial goals.

As we move forward in this book, we will explore the intricacies of money market funds in greater detail, enabling you to make informed decisions and leverage their benefits effectively.

2: ADVANTAGES AND RISKS OF MONEY MARKET FUNDS

W e now delve into the advantages that money market funds offer as well as the potential risks and drawbacks that investors should be aware of before making investment decisions. By gaining insights into both the benefits and potential challenges, you'll be equipped to make informed and prudent choices when it comes to money market fund investments.

THE BENEFITS OF INVESTING IN MONEY MARKET FUNDS:

Safety and Capital Preservation: One of the primary advantages of money market funds is their emphasis on safety and capital preservation. By investing in high-quality, short-term debt instruments, these funds aim to minimize the risk of losing principal, making them a reliable option for safeguarding your cash.

Liquidity and Accessibility: Money market funds provide a high level of liquidity, allowing investors to access their funds quickly and without incurring significant penalties. This liquidity makes them an excellent choice for short-term cash needs or emergency funds.

Stable Returns: While money market funds may not offer sky-high returns, they typically provide a stable and predictable source of income. The consistent income stream can be particularly valuable in uncertain economic environments or when seeking stability in your investment portfolio.

Low Investment Threshold: Money market funds often have low minimum investment requirements, making them accessible to a wide range of investors, including those who are just starting their investment journey.

Diversification: Investing in money market funds can enhance diversification within a portfolio, as they offer a different risk profile compared to other asset classes like stocks and bonds. This diversification can help reduce overall portfolio risk and stabilize returns.

RISKS AND POTENTIAL DRAWBACKS TO CONSIDER

Low Return Potential: While money market funds offer stability and safety, they come with a trade-off in terms of return potential. The yields on money market funds are generally lower than those of riskier investments, such as stocks or long-term bonds.

Inflation Risk: One of the primary risks associated with money market funds is inflation risk. If the fund's returns do not outpace the rate of inflation, the purchasing power of your money could erode over time.

Interest Rate Risk: Money market funds are sensitive to changes in interest rates. When interest rates rise, the yields on new money market investments increase, potentially causing the value of existing fund shares to decrease.

Credit Risk: While money market funds invest in high-quality, short-term debt instruments, there is still a small element of credit risk. If one of the underlying issuers defaults on its obligations, it could impact the fund's performance.

Market Conditions: Money market funds are not immune to market conditions. Although they aim to maintain a stable net asset value (NAV) of $1 per share, there is a slight possibility that a fund's NAV could fall below $1, known as "breaking the buck."

UNDERSTANDING THE IMPACT OF INFLATION AND INTEREST

RATES

Inflation and interest rates are critical factors to consider when investing in money market funds. Inflation erodes the purchasing power of money over time, which means that if the fund's returns do not outpace inflation, your investment's real value may decline.

Furthermore, changes in interest rates can affect the yields of money market funds. When interest rates rise, new money market investments typically offer higher yields, making existing funds with lower yields comparatively less attractive.

As an investor, it is essential to stay informed about economic conditions and interest rate trends, as they can impact the performance of your money market fund investments.

In the next chapter, we will explore the mechanics of how money market funds work, giving you a deeper understanding of their operations and investment strategies.

3: HOW MONEY MARKET FUNDS WORK

In this chapter, we will explore the mechanics of money market funds, gaining insight into their inner workings, the types of money market instruments they invest in, and the fees and expenses associated with these investments. By understanding these crucial aspects, you will be well-equipped to make informed decisions when investing in money market funds.

THE MECHANICS OF MONEY MARKET FUNDS:

Money market funds operate as mutual funds, pooling together money from multiple investors to invest in a diversified portfolio of short-term, low-risk debt instruments. These funds are managed by professional portfolio managers, who make investment decisions based on the fund's stated objectives and investment guidelines.

The goal of money market fund management is to maintain a stable net asset value (NAV) of $1 per share. This means that for every share of the fund, investors expect to receive back at least $1 in value, regardless of market fluctuations.

TYPES OF MONEY MARKET INSTRUMENTS IN THE FUND'S PORTFOLIO:

Money market funds invest in a variety of short-term debt instruments, including but not limited to:

Treasury Bills (T-Bills): Issued by the U.S. government, T-Bills are short-term debt securities with maturities ranging from a few days to one year.

Commercial Paper: Short-term debt issued by corporations to meet their immediate funding needs.

Certificates of Deposit (CDs): Time deposits with fixed maturities offered by banks and financial institutions.

Repurchase Agreements (Repos): Short-term agreements involving the sale and repurchase of securities, often backed by government securities.

Banker's Acceptances: Short-term, time-drawn drafts used to facilitate international trade transactions.

Short-term Municipal Bonds: Debt securities issued by state and local governments with maturities typically less than one year.

These instruments are carefully selected based on their credit quality, maturity, and liquidity to ensure the fund's overall safety and stability.

FEES AND EXPENSES TO WATCH OUT FOR:

When investing in money market funds, it's essential to be aware of the fees and expenses associated with these investments. Common fees include:

Expense Ratio: This fee covers the fund's operating expenses and is expressed as a percentage of the fund's assets. Lower expense ratios can enhance your overall returns.

Management Fee: The management fee compensates the fund's portfolio managers and administrative staff for managing the fund.

12b-1 Fee: This fee covers distribution and marketing expenses. It is typically found in certain share classes of money market funds.

Shareholder Servicing Fee: This fee is charged to cover expenses related to servicing and providing support to shareholders.

While money market funds are generally low-cost investment options, fees can vary among funds and share classes. It's crucial to review the fund's prospectus for a detailed breakdown of all fees and expenses.

Understanding the mechanics of money market funds, the types of instruments they invest in, and the associated fees will enable you to make informed investment decisions aligned with your financial goals.

In the next chapter, we will explore how to assess your financial goals, risk tolerance, and select the right money market fund that suits your individual needs.

PART 2: GETTING STARTED WITH MONEY MARKET FUND INVESTING

4: ASSESSING YOUR FINANCIAL GOALS AND RISK TOLERANCE

To build a strong foundation for financial success, it is crucial to assess your financial goals, understand your risk tolerance, and ensure that your money market fund investments align seamlessly with your comprehensive financial plan. In this chapter, we will guide you through the process of evaluating your objectives and risk appetite, allowing you to make strategic and well-informed decisions when it comes to investing in money market funds.

IDENTIFYING SHORT-TERM FINANCIAL GOALS

Before making any investment decisions, it's crucial to have a clear understanding of your short-term financial goals. These goals could include:

Emergency Fund: Building a fund to cover unexpected expenses or financial emergencies.

Saving for Large Purchases: Funding a down payment for a home, a car, or any other significant purchase you plan to make in the near future.

Vacation Fund: Accumulating money for a dream vacation or travel plans.

Education Expenses: Saving for educational expenses like tuition fees or educational courses.

Short-Term Investment Opportunities: Having cash available to take advantage of time-sensitive investment opportunities.

By identifying and prioritizing your short-term financial goals, you can determine how much money you need to set aside in money market funds or other short-term investments to meet these objectives.

UNDERSTANDING YOUR RISK TOLERANCE AND INVESTMENT HORIZON

Risk tolerance refers to your ability and willingness to endure fluctuations in the value of your investments. To assess your risk tolerance, consider the following factors:

Time Horizon: Evaluate your investment time horizon, which refers to the length of time you can keep your money invested without needing to access it. Longer investment horizons generally allow for more risk-taking.

Financial Situation: Consider your current financial situation, including your income, expenses, debt levels, and other financial commitments.

Emotional Comfort: Reflect on how comfortable you are with potential fluctuations in your investment value. Avoid investing in assets that cause undue stress or anxiety.

Investment Knowledge: Assess your understanding of financial markets and investment concepts. Knowledgeable investors may be more willing to take on higher risks.

ALIGNING MONEY MARKET FUND INVESTMENTS WITH YOUR OVERALL FINANCIAL PLAN

Once you have a clear understanding of your financial goals and risk tolerance, it's time to align your money market fund investments with your overall financial plan:

Emergency Fund: Money market funds are an excellent choice for emergency funds due to their high liquidity and stability. Aim to keep at least three to six months' worth of living expenses in a readily accessible money market fund.

Short-Term Goals: For short-term goals, such as saving for a vacation or making a large purchase within a year, money market funds can provide a safe and reliable place to grow your savings.

Risk Mitigation: Money market funds can serve as a risk-mitigating component in a diversified investment portfolio. They offer stability and liquidity, acting as a cushion during market downturns.

Opportunity Funds: Consider keeping a portion of your investment capital in money market funds or cash equivalents to be ready to take advantage of attractive investment opportunities as they arise.

Money market funds are best suited for short-term goals and preserving capital, rather than seeking high returns. For long-term financial goals, you may need to consider other investment options that offer potential for greater growth.

By carefully aligning your money market fund investments with your financial goals and risk tolerance, you can create a balanced and well-structured investment strategy that supports your journey toward financial security.

In the next chapter, we will explore the process of choosing the right money market fund, taking into account important factors such as fund types, performance, and fees.

5: CHOOSING THE RIGHT MONEY MARKET FUND

Selecting the perfect money market fund to match your financial objectives involves a careful analysis of various factors. By exploring the available options and understanding the key considerations, you can make astute decisions that align with your long-term aspirations.

In this chapter, we will guide you through the process of evaluating different money market fund options and provide valuable insights into the factors to consider when selecting the right fund to suit your financial goals.

EVALUATING DIFFERENT MONEY MARKET FUND OPTIONS:

Money market funds come in various types, each with its unique characteristics. When evaluating different fund options, consider the following:

Government Money Market Funds: These funds invest primarily in U.S. government securities, such as Treasury bills, offering a high level of safety but potentially lower yields compared to other types.

Prime Money Market Funds: These funds invest in a combination of short-term corporate debt and government securities, providing slightly higher yields than government funds but with slightly more risk.

Tax-Exempt Money Market Funds: Suitable for investors in higher tax brackets, these funds invest in short-term municipal securities, providing federal tax-free income.

Retail vs. Institutional Funds: Some money market funds offer different share classes for individual retail investors and institutional investors. Institutional funds may have lower expense ratios but often require higher minimum investments.

FACTORS TO CONSIDER WHEN SELECTING A FUND

Fund Objectives: Ensure that the fund's investment objectives align with your own financial goals and risk tolerance. Some funds may prioritize liquidity, while others aim for higher yields.

Fund Size and Liquidity: Larger funds often benefit from economies of scale, which can lead to lower expense ratios. Additionally, check the fund's liquidity to ensure it can meet redemption demands without significant delays or costs.

Credit Quality: Examine the credit quality of the underlying securities held by the fund. Higher credit quality indicates lower credit risk and increased stability.

Expense Ratio: Compare the expense ratios of different money market funds. Lower expense ratios can enhance your overall returns, especially in a low-interest-rate environment.

Fund Management Team: Research the experience and track record of the fund's management team. A skilled and experienced team can make a difference in navigating changing market conditions.

TIPS FOR COMPARING FUND PERFORMANCE AND FEES

Yield: Compare the yields of different money market funds, but be cautious of funds offering significantly higher yields, as they may be taking on higher risks.

Historical Performance: Review the fund's historical performance over various market conditions. However, remember that past performance is not a guarantee of future results.

Morningstar Ratings: Utilize independent financial research firms like Morningstar to access ratings and analyses of money market funds. These ratings can provide valuable insights into a fund's risk-adjusted performance.

Total Returns: Assess the fund's total returns after accounting for fees and expenses to get a more accurate picture of the fund's performance.

Fee Waivers: Some funds may temporarily waive fees to maintain a stable net asset value (NAV) at $1 per share. Be aware of the terms and duration of these fee waivers.

By conducting thorough research and comparing various money market fund options, you can make an informed decision and choose a fund that aligns with your financial goals and risk tolerance.

In the next chapter, we will explore in more detail, the different money market fund options.

6: GOVERNMENT MONEY MARKET FUNDS

PRESERVING CAPITAL WITH CONFIDENCE

Government Money Market Funds, also known as Treasury Money Market Funds, are a specific type of money market fund that invests primarily in short-term U.S. government securities. These funds focus on providing investors with a combination of safety, liquidity, and competitive yields by investing in debt instruments issued or guaranteed by the U.S. government and its agencies.

UNDERSTANDING GOVERNMENT MONEY MARKET FUNDS

Government Money Market Funds are renowned for their conservative approach to investing. They offer investors a haven of safety and security, backed by the full faith and credit of the U.S. government. These funds aim to preserve capital and provide easy access to liquidity for short-term cash needs.

EXAMPLES OF INVESTMENTS IN GOVERNMENT MONEY MARKET FUNDS

Treasury Bills (T-Bills): As one of the safest investments in the world, T-Bills are short-term debt securities issued by the U.S. Department of the Treasury. With maturities ranging from a few days to one year, T-Bills provide a secure and stable investment option.

Treasury Notes (T-Notes) and Treasury Bonds (T-Bonds): These intermediate and long-term debt securities offer attractive yields while maintaining a high level of safety. T-Notes have maturities ranging from two to ten years, while T-Bonds have longer maturities, typically from ten to thirty years.

Treasury Inflation-Protected Securities (TIPS): TIPS are designed to protect investors from inflation by adjusting their principal value based on changes in the Consumer Price Index (CPI). These securities offer a hedge against the eroding effects of inflation over time.

Federal Agency Securities: Government Money Market Funds may also invest in short-term debt issued by U.S. government agencies, such as Fannie Mae, Freddie Mac, and the Federal Home Loan Banks. These securities have relatively low credit risk due to their government-sponsored status.

Examples of well-known Government Money Market Funds include:

Vanguard Treasury Money Market Fund: This fund is managed by Vanguard, one of the largest and most respected investment management companies globally. The Vanguard Treasury Money Market Fund focuses on investing in U.S. government securities, primarily Treasury bills, providing investors with a low-risk and highly liquid option.

Fidelity Government Money Market Fund: Managed by Fidelity Investments, this fund primarily invests in U.S. government securities, including Treasury bills, notes, and other government agency securities. The Fidelity Government Money Market Fund aims to provide investors with stability and preservation of capital.

Schwab Treasury Obligations Money Market Fund: Offered by Charles Schwab, this fund invests exclusively in U.S. government securities, including Treasury bills, Treasury notes, and other short-term U.S. government obligations. The Schwab Treasury Obligations Money Market Fund aims to provide safety and liquidity to its investors.

BlackRock Treasury Fund: Managed by BlackRock, one of the world's largest asset management firms, this fund focuses on investing in U.S. government securities, including Treasury bills, bonds, and inflation-protected securities. The BlackRock Treasury Fund aims to deliver competitive yields while maintaining a high level of safety.

JPMorgan U.S. Treasury Plus Money Market Fund: Offered by J.P. Morgan Asset Management, this fund invests primarily in U.S. government securities, focusing on Treasury bills and notes. The JPMorgan U.S. Treasury Plus Money Market Fund aims to provide a high level of liquidity and competitive yields to investors.

SAFETY AND LIQUIDITY

One of the key attractions of Government Money Market Funds is their commitment to safety and liquidity. Investors can rest assured that their investments are backed by the U.S. government, making them highly unlikely to default. Additionally, these funds provide daily liquidity, allowing investors to access their money quickly and efficiently.

RISK CONSIDERATIONS

While Government Money Market Funds offer a high level of safety, it's essential to understand that they are not entirely risk-free. They are subject to interest rate risk, which means that fluctuations in interest rates can impact the funds' yields and share prices. Moreover, the returns from these funds might not keep pace with inflation over the long term, making them more suitable for preserving capital rather than generating substantial growth.

SUITABILITY FOR INVESTORS

Government Money Market Funds are ideal for risk-averse investors seeking a stable place to park their cash and meet short-term financial goals. They are particularly well-suited for emergency funds, money set aside for upcoming expenses, or as a temporary parking spot for funds awaiting investment in other asset classes.

Government Money Market Funds offer peace of mind to investors, combining capital preservation with the security of U.S. government backing. By investing in a diverse range of short-term government securities, these funds provide stability and easy access to cash. Whether you're a conservative investor or seeking to balance higher-risk investments in your portfolio, Government Money Market Funds can play a pivotal role in preserving your capital with confidence.

7: PRIME MONEY MARKET FUNDS

BALANCING YIELD AND LIQUIDITY

P rime Money Market Funds is a class of money market funds that aim to strike a balance between yield and liquidity. Unlike Government Money Market Funds, Prime Money Market Funds primarily invest in short-term debt securities issued by corporations and financial institutions, offering slightly higher yields with a modest increase in credit and liquidity risk.

UNDERSTANDING PRIME MONEY MARKET FUNDS

Prime Money Market Funds are designed for investors seeking competitive yields while maintaining a high level of liquidity. These funds invest in a variety of short-term debt instruments issued by corporations, financial institutions, and other entities with strong credit ratings.

EXAMPLES OF INVESTMENTS IN PRIME MONEY MARKET FUNDS

Commercial Paper: Prime Money Market Funds often hold commercial paper, which are short-term debt instruments issued by corporations and financial institutions. Commercial paper typically has maturities ranging from a few days to 270 days.

Bank Certificates of Deposit (CDs): Prime Money Market Funds may invest in certificates of deposit issued by banks. CDs are time deposits with fixed maturities and offer higher yields compared to regular savings accounts.

Bankers' Acceptances: These are short-term financial instruments used to facilitate international trade. Bankers' acceptances are guaranteed by banks and are typically used in import and export transactions.

Repurchase Agreements (Repos): Similar to Government Money Market Funds, Prime Money Market Funds may invest in repurchase agreements, where they purchase securities with an agreement to resell them at a slightly higher price shortly after. Repos are secured by the underlying securities, reducing credit risk.

Examples of prominent Prime Money Market Funds include:

Vanguard Prime Money Market Fund: Managed by Vanguard, this fund focuses on investing in high-quality, short-term debt securities issued by corporations and financial institutions. The Vanguard Prime Money Market Fund aims to provide investors with competitive yields while maintaining liquidity and stability.

Fidelity Prime Money Market Fund: Offered by Fidelity Investments, this fund primarily invests in short-term debt securities issued by domestic and foreign corporations, financial institutions, and other entities. The Fidelity Prime Money Market Fund aims to deliver attractive yields while managing credit risk.

Schwab Value Advantage Money Fund: Managed by Charles Schwab, this fund invests in a diversified portfolio of high-quality, short-term debt securities issued by corporations and financial institutions. The Schwab Value Advantage Money Fund aims to provide investors with current income and capital preservation.

BlackRock Prime Money Market Fund: Managed by BlackRock, one of the world's largest investment management firms, this fund invests in a broad range of high-quality, short-term debt securities, including commercial paper and certificates of deposit. The BlackRock Prime Money Market Fund aims to deliver competitive yields while maintaining a strong focus on safety and liquidity.

JPMorgan Prime Money Market Fund: Offered by J.P. Morgan Asset Management, this fund invests in short-term debt securities issued by U.S. and non-U.S. corporations and financial institutions. The JPMorgan Prime Money Market Fund aims to provide investors with a stable source of income and capital preservation.

BALANCING RISK AND REWARD

Prime Money Market Funds offer a step-up in yield compared to Government Money Market Funds due to their exposure to slightly higher-risk assets. While these funds maintain a focus on capital preservation and liquidity, investors should be aware of the slightly increased credit risk associated with the underlying securities.

SUITABILITY FOR INVESTORS

Prime Money Market Funds are well-suited for investors looking for a balance between safety and higher yields. These funds may be suitable for those with moderate risk tolerance and a desire for additional income generation compared to Government Money Market Funds.

RISK CONSIDERATIONS

Although Prime Money Market Funds hold high-quality, short-term debt securities, they are not entirely risk-free. The creditworthiness of the underlying issuers and changes in interest rates can impact the funds' yields and share prices. Investors should carefully review the credit quality and liquidity of the securities held by the funds.

Prime Money Market Funds offer investors an attractive middle ground, providing competitive yields with a manageable level of credit and liquidity risk. As you evaluate your investment options, consider Prime Money Market Funds as a potential choice for balancing yield and liquidity in your portfolio. By understanding the underlying investments and risk considerations, you can make informed decisions that align with your financial goals and risk tolerance.

8: TAX-EXEMPT MONEY MARKET FUNDS

MAXIMIZING RETURNS WITH TAX EFFICIENCY

Tax-Exempt Money Market Funds is a specialized class of money market funds that offer a unique advantage for investors seeking tax-efficient options. These funds primarily invest in short-term municipal securities issued by state and local governments, providing tax-exempt income at the federal level and often at the state level as well.

UNDERSTANDING TAX-EXEMPT MONEY MARKET FUNDS

Tax-Exempt Money Market Funds are designed to provide investors with competitive yields on their investments while minimizing the impact of taxes. By focusing on short-term municipal securities, these funds aim to generate tax-free income, making them particularly appealing for investors in higher tax brackets.

EXAMPLES OF INVESTMENTS IN TAX-EXEMPT MONEY MARKET FUNDS

Municipal Bonds: Tax-Exempt Money Market Funds primarily invest in municipal bonds issued by state and local governments to fund various public projects. These bonds offer interest payments that are generally exempt from federal income taxes.

State and Local Government Notes: These are short-term debt securities issued by state and local governments to finance short-term needs. Like municipal bonds, the interest on these securities is often exempt from federal income taxes and may also be exempt from state taxes, depending on the investor's state of residence.

Examples of notable Tax-Exempt Money Market Funds include:

Vanguard Tax-Exempt Money Market Fund: Managed by Vanguard, this fund invests in short-term municipal securities issued by state and local governments. The Vanguard Tax-Exempt Money Market Fund aims to provide tax-free income at the federal level, making it attractive for investors seeking to reduce their federal tax liabilities.

Fidelity Tax-Exempt Money Market Fund: Offered by Fidelity Investments, this fund primarily invests in short-term municipal securities to generate tax-exempt income at the federal level. The Fidelity Tax-Exempt Money Market Fund aims to provide a high level of tax efficiency for investors in higher tax brackets.

Schwab Tax-Free Money Fund: Managed by Charles Schwab, this fund invests in short-term municipal securities issued by state and local governments. The Schwab Tax-Free Money Fund seeks to offer federal and sometimes state tax-exempt income, making it suitable for investors looking to minimize their tax burden.

BlackRock Tax-Exempt Money Market Fund: Managed by BlackRock, this fund focuses on investing in short-term municipal securities to provide investors with tax-exempt income at the federal level. The BlackRock Tax-Exempt Money Market Fund aims to deliver competitive yields while maintaining a focus on tax efficiency.

JPMorgan Tax-Free Money Market Fund: Offered by J.P. Morgan Asset Management, this fund invests in a diversified portfolio of short-term municipal securities issued by state and local governments. The JPMorgan Tax-Free Money Market Fund aims to provide tax-free income to investors seeking to preserve their capital while reducing their tax liability.

TAX EFFICIENCY AND AFTER-TAX RETURNS

One of the main advantages of Tax-Exempt Money Market Funds is their potential for tax efficiency. By investing in tax-exempt securities, these funds allow investors to keep a higher percentage of their income, especially compared to taxable money market funds. As a result, investors may achieve higher after-tax returns, particularly if they are subject to higher federal tax rates.

RISK CONSIDERATIONS

While Tax-Exempt Money Market Funds offer tax advantages, investors should be aware that they still carry some level of risk. The credit quality of the municipal securities held by these funds can vary, and changes in interest rates can impact the funds' yields and share prices. It's essential to carefully review the credit quality and diversification of the underlying securities before making investment decisions.

SUITABILITY FOR INVESTORS

Tax-Exempt Money Market Funds are particularly attractive to investors in higher tax brackets who seek to minimize their tax liability while earning competitive returns. Additionally, they may be beneficial for investors looking to achieve short-term financial goals with the added benefit of tax efficiency.

Tax-Exempt Money Market Funds offer a compelling opportunity to enhance returns through tax efficiency while preserving capital and maintaining liquidity. For investors in higher tax brackets, these funds can be a valuable addition to their investment portfolio. By understanding the tax advantages and underlying securities, you can make informed decisions to maximize your after-tax returns while achieving your financial objectives.

9: RETAIL VS. INSTITUTIONAL MONEY MARKET FUNDS
UNDERSTANDING THE KEY DIFFERENCES

R etail and Institutional Money Market Funds are two cat-egories of money market funds that cater to different types of investors. While both types share similar invest-ment objectives, they differ in terms of minimum investment re-quirements, fees, and access to specific features. Understanding the characteristics of each fund type will empower you to choose the one that best aligns with your investment needs and financial goals.

RETAIL MONEY MARKET FUNDS

Retail Money Market Funds are designed for individual investors seeking easy accessibility and flexibility. These funds typically have lower minimum investment requirements, making them more accessible to a wide range of investors. Retail funds may offer additional features, such as check-writing privileges, which allow investors to conveniently access their funds.

EXAMPLES OF RETAIL MONEY MARKET FUND FEATURES

Lower Minimum Investment: Retail Money Market Funds often have lower initial investment thresholds, making them attractive to individual investors who want to start with a smaller amount.

Check-Writing Privileges: Some retail funds may offer check-writing capabilities, enabling investors to write checks directly from their money market fund accounts for ease of use in paying bills or making purchases.

Retail Investor-Focused: Retail funds are marketed to individual investors and may be available through various financial institutions, including banks, brokerages, and mutual fund companies.

INSTITUTIONAL MONEY MARKET FUNDS

Institutional Money Market Funds cater to larger investors, such as corporations, institutions, and high-net-worth individuals. These funds often have higher minimum investment requirements and may offer more institutional-oriented services, but they typically have lower expense ratios compared to retail funds.

EXAMPLES OF INSTITUTIONAL MONEY MARKET FUND FEATURES

Higher Minimum Investment: Institutional Money Market Funds generally require larger initial investments, making them more suitable for institutional investors with significant capital to deploy.

Lower Expense Ratios: Due to the larger investment size of institutional clients, these funds can negotiate lower expense ratios, resulting in potentially higher net returns for investors.

Institutional Client-Focused: Institutional funds are tailored to meet the needs of corporations, organizations, and high-net-worth individuals, often available through specialized investment firms and platforms.

SUITABILITY FOR INVESTORS

The choice between Retail and Institutional Money Market Funds depends on individual circumstances and investment preferences. Retail funds are well-suited for individual investors seeking easy accessibility and flexibility, while Institutional funds are better suited for larger investors looking for potential cost savings and services tailored to their specific needs.

Understanding the differences between Retail and Institutional Money Market Funds is vital to making informed investment decisions. Whether you are an individual investor or represent an organization, choosing the right fund type can significantly impact your overall investment experience. By weighing the features, minimum investment requirements, and expenses associated with each fund type, you can select the one that aligns perfectly with your financial goals and investment preferences.

10: OPENING AN INVESTMENT ACCOUNT

Navigating the process of opening an investment account can seem daunting. Let's look at the steps involved and equip you with the knowledge needed to make informed decisions, whether you choose a brokerage account or opt for a direct account with a mutual fund company. In this chapter, we will guide you through the process of opening an investment account, providing insights into different account options and the steps to set up a money market fund account.

EXPLORING DIFFERENT ACCOUNT OPTIONS

When it comes to opening an investment account to invest in money market funds, you have a few options to consider:

Brokerage Accounts: Many brokerage firms offer a wide range of investment products, including money market funds. Opening a brokerage account gives you access to various funds from different fund families, providing flexibility and diversity in your investment choices. However, be mindful of brokerage fees and commissions that may apply.

Mutual Fund Company Accounts: Some investors prefer to open accounts directly with mutual fund companies. This option allows you to invest directly in their money market funds without incurring brokerage fees. Additionally, it simplifies the investment process, as you deal directly with the fund provider.

Retirement Accounts: If your investment goals align with retirement savings, consider utilizing tax-advantaged retirement accounts like Individual Retirement Accounts (IRAs) or employer-sponsored retirement plans (e.g., 401(k)s). Many of these accounts offer money market fund options, providing a stable and safe choice for your retirement savings.

THE PROCESS OF SETTING UP A MONEY MARKET FUND ACCOUNT

The process of setting up a money market fund account is relatively straightforward:

Research and Choose the Fund: Determine the money market fund that best aligns with your financial goals and risk tolerance. Consider the factors mentioned in Chapter 5 to make an informed decision.

Gather Required Documents: When opening an investment account, you may need to provide identification documents, such as a valid ID, social security number, and proof of address. Be prepared with these documents to expedite the account setup process.

Complete the Application: Whether you choose a brokerage account or a mutual fund company account, you'll need to complete an account application. This application will collect essential information, such as your contact details, investment objectives, and risk tolerance.

Funding Your Account: After your account is approved, you'll need to fund it. You can do this by transferring money from your bank account or from an existing investment account.

NAVIGATING ACCOUNT MINIMUMS AND FEES

Different money market funds and account providers may have varying minimum investment requirements and fee structures. Here's what to consider:

Account Minimums: Some money market funds and investment accounts may have minimum initial investment requirements. Ensure you meet these minimums before proceeding with the account setup.

Fees and Expenses: Be aware of any fees associated with the account, such as transaction fees, account maintenance fees, or expense ratios. Compare these fees across different account options to select the most cost-effective one.

Fee Waivers: Some fund providers may offer fee waivers or discounts based on account size or other criteria. Be sure to inquire about any fee waivers that may apply to your investment account.

By carefully selecting the right investment account option, understanding the account setup process, and navigating fees and minimums, you can efficiently open an investment account and start investing in money market funds to achieve your financial goals.

In the next chapter, we will explore strategies for boosting returns on your money market fund investments and optimizing your portfolio.

PART 3: MAXIMIZING RETURNS AND MANAGING RISKS

11: STRATEGIES FOR BOOSTING RETURNS

L et's dive into an array of powerful strategies that will enable you to unlock the full potential of your money market fund investments and elevate your overall portfolio performance. While money market funds are known for their stability and liquidity, there are several smart approaches that can help you enhance your returns without compromising on safety.

From reinvestment options that can compound your earnings to utilizing sweep accounts for added convenience, we will unveil a plethora of tactics designed to optimize the growth of your investments.

With an informed understanding of these strategies, you can make your money work harder for you, ensuring that every dollar you invest thrives to its fullest potential.

REINVESTMENT OPTIONS FOR MONEY MARKET FUND DIVIDENDS

Money market funds generate income through dividends from the interest earned on their underlying securities. Instead of withdrawing these dividends, consider reinvesting them to compound your returns. Reinvesting dividends can accelerate the growth of your investment over time, as the reinvested dividends themselves start earning additional dividends.

Many money market funds offer dividend reinvestment plans

(DRIPs), allowing you to automatically reinvest your dividends to purchase additional fund shares. By reinvesting dividends, you take advantage of the power of compounding and potentially boost the overall return on your investment.

UTILIZING SWEEP ACCOUNTS FOR ADDED CONVENIENCE

Some brokerage firms and financial institutions offer sweep accounts that provide added convenience and the potential for higher returns. Sweep accounts automatically transfer any excess cash in your brokerage account into a higher-yielding money market fund or cash equivalent.

By using a sweep account, you ensure that your idle cash is continuously invested in a money market fund, earning returns until you decide to utilize the funds for other investments or withdraw them for spending purposes. Sweep accounts help you optimize returns while maintaining liquidity and accessibility.

LADDERING AND OTHER STRATEGIES TO OPTIMIZE RETURNS

Laddering: Laddering is a strategy that involves dividing your investment into multiple money market funds with varying maturities. For example, instead of investing all your funds in a single money market fund, you allocate them into funds with maturities of three months, six months, and one year.

With laddering, you benefit from the flexibility of having funds maturing at different intervals. As shorter-term funds mature, you can reinvest them at potentially higher interest rates, taking advantage of rising rates in the market.

Barbelling: Barbelling is another strategy where you concentrate your investments at both ends of the yield curve. This involves allocating funds to short-term money market funds with lower interest rate risk and long-term money market funds with potentially higher yields.

Sector Rotation: If you're using a brokerage account with access to various money market funds, consider rotating your investments between different sectors or fund types based on changing market conditions. Sector rotation allows you to respond to shifts in interest rates and economic trends.

Stay Informed: Regularly monitor economic indicators and interest rate trends to make informed decisions about when to adjust your money market fund investments.

Money market funds are generally considered safe and stable, and their primary goal is capital preservation. While these strategies can help optimize returns, they may involve varying degrees of risk and require careful consideration based on your financial goals and risk tolerance.

In the next chapter, we will focus on monitoring your money market fund portfolio and knowing when to adjust your investment strategy to ensure continued financial security.

12: MONITORING YOUR MONEY MARKET FUND PORTFOLIO

While money market funds are renowned for their stability, vigilant monitoring of your investments remains a key aspect of a thriving portfolio. We will equip you with the tools to assess fund performance, track changes, and understand the indicators that call for adjustments to your investment strategy.

Just as a skilled captain navigates a ship to its destination, you too can navigate your financial ship towards prosperity. With the knowledge gained in this chapter, you will have the confidence to make timely and informed decisions, ensuring your money market fund investments are on course to accomplish your financial goals.

THE IMPORTANCE OF REGULAR PORTFOLIO REVIEW

Regularly reviewing your money market fund portfolio is crucial to ensure that it remains aligned with your financial goals and risk tolerance. The financial landscape can change rapidly, and staying informed about market conditions and economic trends will help you make informed decisions about your investments.

Set a schedule for periodic portfolio reviews, taking into account your investment horizon and the frequency of market changes. A systematic review process allows you to identify any deviations from your initial investment plan and make necessary adjustments.

ASSESSING THE FUND'S PERFORMANCE AND TRACKING CHANGES

When evaluating your money market fund's performance, consider the following:

Yield and Return: Compare the fund's yield and total return against its peers and relevant benchmarks. This will give you an idea of how well the fund is performing relative to other similar funds.

Expense Ratio: Review the fund's expense ratio to ensure that it remains competitive and cost-effective.

Consistency: Look for consistency in the fund's returns over time. A stable and reliable income stream is essential for money market funds.

Fund Manager's Performance: Evaluate the fund manager's track record and how they have navigated different market conditions.

Interest Rate Environment: Consider the current interest rate environment and how it may impact the fund's performance.

KNOWING WHEN TO ADJUST YOUR INVESTMENT STRATEGY

There are several scenarios that may prompt you to adjust your money market fund investment strategy:

Changing Financial Goals: If your financial goals or risk tolerance have changed, your investment strategy should reflect these updates.

Market Conditions: Changes in interest rates, economic indicators, or market trends may impact money market fund performance. Stay informed about market conditions and adjust your strategy accordingly.

Fund Performance: If a money market fund consistently underperforms compared to its peers or benchmarks, you may consider reallocating to a better-performing fund.

Interest Rate Changes: In an environment of rising interest rates, consider laddering or reallocating to capture higher yields as short-term funds mature.

Portfolio Rebalancing: Periodically rebalance your portfolio to ensure that your asset allocation remains consistent with your investment goals.

Always make adjustments to your investment strategy thoughtfully and avoid making hasty decisions based on short-term market fluctuations. Consult with a financial advisor if you need guidance on rebalancing or adjusting your portfolio.

The goal of monitoring your money market fund portfolio is to maintain a well-aligned and diversified investment strategy that supports your long-term financial security.

In the next chapter, we will explore the tax considerations related to money market fund investing and strategies for enhancing after-tax returns.

PART 4: ADVANCED MONEY MARKET FUND CONCEPTS

13: TAX CONSIDERATIONS AND MONEY MARKET FUNDS

While money market funds offer stability and liquidity, the tax treatment of your investments can significantly impact your after-tax returns. We will guide you through the nuances of tax-efficient strategies, enabling you to retain more of your hard-earned income and potentially achieve higher net returns.

As you explore the tax implications of money market funds, you will discover how to minimize your tax liability, make the most of available tax benefits, and align your investment choices with your overall tax planning. By mastering these essential tax insights, you can ensure that your money market fund investments work optimally for you and take your financial journey to greater heights.

UNDERSTANDING THE TAX IMPLICATIONS OF MONEY MARKET FUND INVESTING

Money market funds can have different tax treatments based on the types of securities they hold and the account in which they are held. Here are some key tax considerations:

Taxable vs. Tax-Exempt Funds: Money market funds can be either taxable or tax-exempt. Taxable funds invest in securities subject to federal income tax, while tax-exempt funds invest in municipal securities that offer federal tax-free income. Tax-exempt funds may also provide tax benefits at the state level, depending on your state of residence.

Taxable Account: If you hold money market funds in a taxable brokerage account, any dividends or interest income earned by the fund may be subject to federal and state income taxes in the year they are received.

Tax-Advantaged Accounts: If you hold money market funds in tax-advantaged accounts, such as Individual Retirement Accounts (IRAs) or employer-sponsored retirement plans like 401(k)s, you can defer taxes on any earnings until you make withdrawals during retirement. Roth IRAs may offer tax-free withdrawals if certain conditions are met.

Capital Gains Taxes: Money market funds may generate capital gains if the fund's portfolio manager buys and sells securities within the fund. These capital gains can be subject to capital gains taxes if you sell your shares at a profit.

TAX-EFFICIENT STRATEGIES TO ENHANCE RETURNS

To enhance after-tax returns when investing in money market funds, consider the following tax-efficient strategies:

Tax-Exempt Funds: If you are in a high tax bracket, consider investing in tax-exempt money market funds. The interest income from these funds is generally exempt from federal income tax and may be exempt from state income tax, providing higher after-tax returns.

Qualified Dividends and Capital Gains: In taxable brokerage accounts, preferentially invest in money market funds that focus on generating qualified dividends and long-term capital gains. These types of income may be taxed at a lower rate than ordinary income.

Asset Location: Consider asset location strategies by holding tax-efficient investments, such as money market funds, in taxable accounts, while keeping tax-inefficient assets, like high-yield bonds or actively traded funds, in tax-advantaged accounts.

Tax Loss Harvesting: In taxable accounts, take advantage of tax loss harvesting opportunities by selling money market fund shares at a loss to offset capital gains from other investments and potentially reduce your tax liability.

Hold-to-Maturity Strategy: If you invest in individual money market instruments directly, consider holding them until maturity. By doing so, you can avoid potential capital gains taxes from changes in the market value of the instrument.

Before implementing any tax-efficient strategies, it's essential to consult with a tax professional or financial advisor who can tailor these strategies to your specific financial situation and objectives.

By understanding the tax implications and employing tax-efficient strategies, you can enhance your overall after-tax returns when investing in money market funds.

In the next chapter, we will provide a summary of key takeaways from this book and offer some final thoughts to help you navigate your money market fund investing journey successfully.

14: DIVERSIFICATION AND ASSET ALLOCATION

Diversification is a time-tested principle that emphasizes the importance of spreading your investments across various asset classes to mitigate risk. Asset allocation, on the other hand, involves strategically distributing your investments among different asset classes based on your financial goals, risk tolerance, and investment horizon.

In this chapter, we explore how money market funds can play a vital role in your asset allocation strategy. As a cornerstone of stability and liquidity, money market funds can serve as a valuable anchor, providing a secure foundation for your investment portfolio.

By harnessing the power of diversification and asset allocation, you can create a portfolio that withstands market fluctuations, maintains liquidity, and aligns with your financial objectives. We will guide you on optimizing the integration of money market funds within your asset allocation framework, ensuring your investment strategy is robust and well-prepared for whatever the market brings.

DIVERSIFYING YOUR INVESTMENT PORTFOLIO WITH MONEY MARKET FUNDS

Diversification is a fundamental principle of investing, aiming to spread your investments across different asset classes to reduce risk and enhance overall returns. Money market funds play a unique role in diversification by providing a safe and stable option for parking cash and preserving capital.

While money market funds are low-risk and provide liquidity, they offer modest returns. Including them in your portfolio allows you to balance higher-risk assets, such as stocks or long-term bonds, with a stable and low-risk investment.

INTEGRATING MONEY MARKET FUNDS INTO A COMPREHENSIVE ASSET ALLOCATION PLAN

When creating an asset allocation plan, consider your financial goals, risk tolerance, and investment horizon. Your asset allocation should reflect your individual circumstances and be aligned with your long-term objectives.

A well-diversified asset allocation may include a mix of:

Money Market Funds: For short-term cash needs, emergency funds, and capital preservation.

Equities (Stocks): For long-term growth potential, although they come with higher volatility.

Fixed-Income (Bonds): For stable income and capital preservation, with lower volatility than equities.

Real Estate: For potential inflation hedging and diversification.

Other Alternatives: Depending on your risk appetite, you might consider other assets like commodities or precious metals.

BALANCING RISK AND REWARD ACROSS DIFFERENT INVESTMENT OPTIONS

The key to successful asset allocation is finding the right balance between risk and reward. Different asset classes have varying levels of risk and potential returns. For example:

Money Market Funds: Low risk, low return. Suitable for preserving capital and providing liquidity.

Equities (Stocks): Higher risk, higher return potential. Suited for long-term growth and capital appreciation.

Fixed-Income (Bonds): Moderate risk, moderate return. Ideal for generating income and providing stability.

Real Estate: Can provide a hedge against inflation and potentially offer attractive returns.

It's essential to periodically rebalance your portfolio to maintain the desired asset allocation as the performance of different asset classes fluctuates over time. Regular rebalancing ensures that your risk exposure stays within your comfort zone and helps you stay on track with your financial goals.

Remember that investment decisions should be based on careful research, long-term planning, and a deep understanding of your financial goals. Be patient and disciplined in your approach to investing, and seek advice from financial professionals when needed.

PART 5: LONG-TERM FINANCIAL SECURITY AND BEYOND

15: TRANSITIONING FROM MONEY MARKET FUNDS

L et's explore the importance of recognizing when it may be time to explore other investment options beyond money market funds and how to strategically reallocate your funds for long-term financial goals. While money market funds offer stability and liquidity, there comes a time in every investor's journey when they may seek to embrace new opportunities for growth and potential higher returns.

We will guide you through the indicators that signal the need for a transition and equip you with the tools to make informed decisions.

Transitioning from money market funds involves carefully assessing your financial goals, risk tolerance, and investment time horizon. By understanding your changing needs and objectives, you can confidently reallocate your funds into investment vehicles that align better with your long-term aspirations.

As you embark on this chapter, you will gain the insights needed to navigate the transition process smoothly. By combining your understanding of money market funds with newfound knowledge of other investment options, you can craft a well-rounded and dynamic portfolio tailored to your evolving financial needs.

WHEN TO CONSIDER OTHER INVESTMENT OPTIONS

While money market funds offer safety, liquidity, and stability, there are situations when it may be appropriate to consider other investment options:

Long-Term Financial Goals: If your financial goals have shifted towards long-term growth and wealth accumulation, money market funds may not provide the desired level of returns. In such cases, you may consider gradually transitioning to other investment options that offer higher growth potential, such as equities (stocks) or equity mutual funds.

Higher Risk Tolerance: As your risk tolerance increases or your financial situation evolves, you may be willing to take on more risk to pursue higher returns. Diversifying your portfolio with a mix of asset classes can help achieve your desired risk-reward balance.

Inflation Hedge: Money market funds may not provide effective protection against inflation over the long term. To combat the eroding effect of inflation on your purchasing power, you might explore investments like real estate, inflation-protected securities, or commodities.

Retirement Planning: For retirement planning, consider a mix of assets that provide a balance between growth potential and capital preservation. Retirement accounts like IRAs and 401(k)s often offer a wide range of investment options to cater to your specific retirement goals.

HOW TO REALLOCATE FUNDS FOR LONG-TERM GOALS

When reallocating funds from money market funds to other investments for long-term goals, follow these steps:

Review Your Goals: Reassess your financial goals, investment horizon, and risk tolerance. Clarify what you want to achieve with your investments in the long term.

Asset Allocation: Determine an appropriate asset allocation that aligns with your goals and risk tolerance. This may involve diversifying your portfolio across different asset classes, such as equities, fixed-income securities, and other investment options.

Gradual Transition: Rather than making abrupt changes, consider a gradual transition from money market funds to other investments. This approach allows you to spread out the risk and potential market timing effects.

Consult a Financial Advisor: Seek guidance from a financial advisor who can help you design a personalized investment strategy based on your unique circumstances and goals.

Monitor and Adjust: Regularly monitor your portfolio's performance and adjust your asset allocation as needed. Rebalance your portfolio periodically to maintain the desired allocation and stay on track with your long-term goals.

Remember that every investor's journey is different, and there is no one-size-fits-all approach to investing. The right investment strategy depends on your individual financial situation, goals, and risk tolerance.

As you transition from money market funds to other investment options, always be mindful of your financial objectives and consider your risk tolerance. By diversifying your portfolio and aligning your investments with your long-term goals, you can work towards building a robust and resilient financial future.

16: BUILDING LASTING FINANCIAL SECURITY

Welcome to the final chapter of Investing in Money Market Funds 101. In this concluding segment, we delve into the crucial role money market funds play in your overall financial journey, and we emphasize the paramount importance of financial education and planning for long-term prosperity.

As we conclude this journey together, we encourage you to continue your financial education and embrace the power of long-term planning. By combining the strength of money market funds with a well-considered financial roadmap, you can pave the way to a secure and prosperous financial future.

UNDERSTANDING THE ROLE OF MONEY MARKET FUNDS IN YOUR FINANCIAL JOURNEY

Money market funds play a vital role in providing stability, liquidity, and capital preservation within your investment portfolio. As a safe haven for short-term cash needs and emergency funds, money market funds offer peace of mind and financial security.

While money market funds are essential for preserving capital and managing short-term financial goals, it's essential to recognize that they are not designed for substantial long-term growth. As your financial journey progresses and your goals evolve, you may need to explore other investment options to achieve higher returns and meet long-term objectives.

INCORPORATING FINANCIAL EDUCATION AND PLANNING FOR LONG-TERM SUCCESS

Financial education and planning are crucial components of building lasting financial security. Here are some essential steps to consider:

Set Clear Financial Goals: Define your short-term and long-term financial goals. Understand the amount of money you need to achieve these goals and the timeframes involved.

Create a Budget: Develop a budget to track your income and expenses. This will help you manage your finances effectively, save more, and invest wisely.

Establish an Emergency Fund: Build an emergency fund with at least three to six months' worth of living expenses in a money market fund or other accessible, low-risk accounts. An emergency fund provides a safety net during unexpected financial hardships.

Pay off High-Interest Debt: Prioritize paying off high-interest debts, such as credit card debt, to reduce financial burdens and increase available funds for investing.

Diversify Your Investment Portfolio: As your financial situation allows, diversify your investment portfolio across various asset classes, including stocks, bonds, real estate, and other alternatives. Diversification helps spread risk and provides the potential for higher returns.

Regularly Review and Reassess: Conduct periodic reviews of your financial plan and investment portfolio. Life circumstances and market conditions change, and it's crucial to adjust your strategies accordingly.

Seek Professional Guidance: Consider working with a financial advisor who can provide personalized advice, tailor investment strategies to your goals, and assist you in making informed financial decisions.

Invest in Financial Education: Continuously seek to enhance your financial literacy. Attend workshops, read books, and stay informed about personal finance, investing, and economic trends.

Building lasting financial security requires a combination of financial discipline, education, and thoughtful planning. Money market funds offer an essential component of capital preservation and liquidity in your investment journey. As your financial goals evolve and your wealth grows, expanding your investment horizons and exploring various asset classes will be key to achieving long-term financial success.

By cultivating good financial habits, making informed investment decisions, and seeking professional guidance when needed, you can create a solid foundation for your financial future. Remember, financial security is a journey, and with dedication and prudent planning, you can work towards realizing your dreams and achieving lasting financial well-being.

CONCLUSION
THE ROAD TO FINANCIAL SECURITY

Congratulations on completing "Money Market Funds Investing 101." In this book, we have explored the fundamentals of money market fund investing, the role of money market funds in a diversified portfolio, and the strategies for building financial security. As we conclude this journey, let's recap the key concepts covered and offer encouragement for taking control of your financial future.

RECAP OF KEY CONCEPTS COVERED IN THE BOOK

Money Market Funds: Money market funds are low-risk mutual funds that invest in short-term, highly liquid, and safe financial instruments, offering stability and capital preservation.

Benefits of Money Market Funds: Money market funds provide a safe haven for short-term cash needs, emergency funds, and capital preservation, making them ideal for risk-averse investors.

Diversification and Asset Allocation: Diversifying your investment portfolio across various asset classes, including money market funds, equities, bonds, and more, helps manage risk and optimize returns.

Assessing Financial Goals and Risk Tolerance: Identifying your short-term financial goals and understanding your risk tolerance are essential steps in aligning your investments with your unique needs.

Choosing the Right Money Market Fund: Evaluating different money market fund options, considering factors such as fund objectives, fees, and management team, aids in making informed investment decisions.

Monitoring Your Portfolio: Regularly reviewing your money market fund portfolio and tracking its performance allows you to stay on track with your financial goals and make necessary adjustments.

Tax Considerations: Understanding the tax implications of money market fund investing and employing tax-efficient strategies can enhance after-tax returns.

Now that you have gained a deeper understanding of money market funds and the principles of sound investing, I encourage you to take control of your financial future. Investing wisely and building financial security are empowering journeys that require dedication, discipline, and ongoing education.

Building wealth and financial security is a gradual process. Start by setting clear financial goals and creating a plan to achieve them. Embrace the power of compounding, where even small, consistent contributions to your investments can grow significantly over time.

Don't be discouraged by market fluctuations or short-term challenges. Stay focused on your long-term objectives and maintain a balanced and diversified portfolio that aligns with your risk tolerance and financial aspirations.

INVESTING WISELY AND BUILDING FINANCIAL SECURITY

Investing wisely is not just about accumulating wealth; it's about securing your financial future, achieving financial independence, and pursuing your dreams. Building financial security provides peace of mind, enabling you to weather economic uncertainties and unforeseen life events.

As you embark on this journey, remain committed to your financial goals and stay informed about economic trends and investment opportunities. Seek professional advice when needed, but always remember that you are the captain of your financial ship, making decisions that shape your future.

Take the knowledge and insights gained from this book and apply them to create a solid financial foundation. Empower yourself with financial literacy, and make informed decisions that align with your values and aspirations.

Best wishes in your journey to financial success and security. May this book serve as a stepping stone on your path to prosperity and a fulfilling financial future.

ABOUT THE AUTHOR

Usiere Uko

Usiere Uko is a Consultant, ILO Certified Trainer, and Business & Finance Author focused on financial independence and entrepreneurship. A former oil and gas engineer turned entrepreneur, he helps individuals and business owners build sustainable income, make smarter financial decisions, and grow resilient businesses.

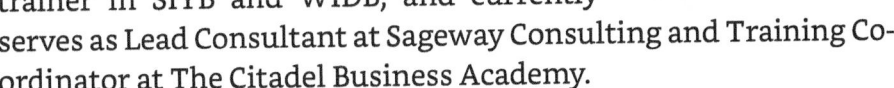

He is a certified Business Development Service Provider (BDSP) and an ILO-certified trainer in SIYB and WIDB, and currently serves as Lead Consultant at Sageway Consulting and Training Coordinator at The Citadel Business Academy.

Usiere writes in a friendly and practical style, making complex financial and business ideas simple, clear, and actionable for everyday readers and entrepreneurs. He is based in Lagos, Nigeria.

BOOKS IN THIS SERIES

SMART INVESTING 101

Money Market Investing 101: A Beginner's Guide To Low-Risk Short-Term Investments

Treasury Bill Investing 101: Your Essential Step-By-Step Guide To Building Financial Security

Treasury Bonds Investing 101: A Beginner's Guide To Low-Risk Investment Strategies

Treasury Notes Investing 101: Step-By-Step Guide And Smart Investor Starter's Handbook

Investing In Tips 101: A Beginner's Guide To Treasury Inflation-Protected Securities

Investing In Money Market Funds 101: The Beginner's Smart Investors Guide To Building Financial Security

Mutual Funds Investing 101: A Beginner's Guide To Building Wealth Through Smart Investing

Stock Market Investing 101: A Practical Beginners Guide To Online And Offline Stock Trading

Making Money With Life Insurance: Simple Strategies For Growing Wealth As A Beginner

Forex For Non-Traders: A Step-By-Step Guide To Earning Forex Income Without Trading

Investing In Peer-To-Peer Lending: A Beginner's Guide To Generating Passive Income Through Crowdlending Platforms

Investing In Etfs 101: A Beginner's Guide For Building Wealth With Exchange-Traded Funds

Nft Investing 101: A Beginner's Guide To Collectible Digital Assets

BOOKS BY THIS AUTHOR

Practical Steps To Financial Freedom And Independence: Money Management Skills For Beginners

Before You Trade Forex: Things You Need To Know If You Desire To Start Trading Forex Profitably

Before You Invest In Cryptocurrency: A Simple Guide To Understanding The Cryptocurrency Market

101 Common Money Mistakes To Avoid: And How To Fix Them. Book 1: Expenses. Money Management, Making Your Budget Work

How To Avoid Living Under Financial Pressure: A Simple Guide To Getting Back Control Of Your Finances

Financial Independence For Employees: Making Your Job A Stepping Stone To Exiting The Rat Race

And Living Your Dreams

Managing Your Money Post Covid: Financial Management Skills For An Era Of High Inflation And Market Disruption

Retire On Your Own Terms: A Simple Guide To Financially Literate Retirement Planning

Your Ultimate Money Makeover: Manage Your Money Better, Take Control Of Your Finances And Your Life

Teaching Kids Money 101: Simple Parenting Strategies For Raising Financially Literate Kids From Toddler To Teen Years And Beyond

Uncle Ben's Money Lessons: Book I: Do You Want To Work For Money? A Vacation Story With An Adventure Into The World Of Money

Nft Investing 101: A Beginner's Guide To Collectible Digital Assets

Stock Market Investing 101: A Practical Beginners Guide To Online And Offline Stock Trading

Investing In Etfs 101: A Beginner's Guide For Building Wealth With Exchange-Traded Funds

Day Trading 101: A Complete Beginner's Guide To Trading The Markets

Forex Trading 101: A Beginner's Guide And Strategies To Profitable Currency Trading

Options Trading 101: A Beginner's Guide To Trading Stock Options

Futures Trading 101: A Step-By-Step Guide And Strategies For Beginner Traders

www.ingramcontent.com/pod-product-compliance
Lightning Source LLC
Chambersburg PA
CBHW070123230526
45472CB00004B/1398